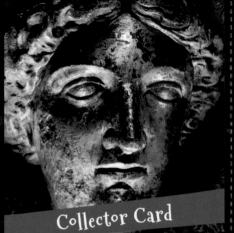

REMARKABLE ROMANS

Collector Card

REMARKABLE ROMANS

Collector Card

REMARKABLE ROMANS

Collector Card

REMARKABLE ROMANS

Collector Card

The road

The Romans built a network of straight roads for travel around their empire.

SCORE

IN USE TODAY: roads in Europe	10
IMPORTANCE: good connections	9
WORLD FIRST: no, but vastly improved	6
ROMAN FIRST: 500BCE	9

Concrete

Concrete was invented for building projects such as Rome's Pantheon.

SCORE

IN USE TODAY: many buildings	9
IMPORTANCE: very useful	7
WORLD FIRST: underwater concrete	10
ROMAN FIRST: cement c. 300BCE	7

The aqueduct

Aqueducts of buried channels and arched bridges carried water to towns.

SCORE

IN USE TODAY: modern aqueducts	7
IMPORTANCE: essential	10
WORLD FIRST: no, but improved	5

The arch

The Romans built curved arches to create strong buildings and bridges.

SCORE

IN USE TODAY: Roman remains	8
IMPORTANCE: design and material use	6
WORLD FIRST: no, but effective use	4

It's all about . . .

REMARKABLE ROMANS

KINGFISHER
NEW YORK

KINGFISHER
LONDON & NEW YORK

Copyright © Macmillan Publishers International Ltd 2017
Published in the United States by Kingfisher,
175 Fifth Ave., New York, NY 10010
Kingfisher is an imprint of Macmillan Children's Books, London
All rights reserved.

Distributed in the U.S. and Canada by Macmillan,
175 Fifth Ave., New York, NY 10010

Library of Congress Cataloging-in-Publication data
has been applied for.

Series editor: Sarah Snashall
Series design: Anthony Hannant (LittleRedAnt)
Adapted from an original text by Philip Steele

ISBN 978-0-7534-7282-8

Kingfisher books are available for special promotions
and premiums. For details contact: Special Markets
Department, Macmillan, 175 Fifth Ave.,
New York, NY 10010.

For more information, please visit
www.kingfisherbooks.com

Printed in China

9 8 7 6 5 4 3 2 1

1TR/0916/WKT/UG/128MA

Picture credits
The Publisher would like to thank the following for permission to reproduce their material.
Top = t; Bottom = b; Center = c; Left = l; Right = r
Cover Alamy/David Cole; back cover iStock/claudiodivizia; pages 1 Alamy/David Cole;
2–3 Shutterstock/Mapics; 4 Shutterstock/Bertl123; 5 Shutterstock/oksmit; 5c Musée de Laon/
Vassil; 6 iStock/Duncan Walker; 6b Shutterstock/saiko3p; 7 Shutterstock/Brian Maudsley;
7t iStock/Cristofolux; 8 iStock/JSSIII; 8c iStock/David Ward; 9b, 10, 12 Kingfisher Artbank;
11 iStock/AndreaAstes; 11t iStock/Hedda Gjerpen; 12b Getty/DEA/M Carrieri; 13 Shutterstock/
Luciano Mortula; 13c Shutterstock/Mapics; 14–15 Shutterstock/Leonid Andronov;
16–17 Kingfisher Artbank; 17t Crodrin.B; 18l Alamy/Lanmas; 18r Joanbanjo; 19l Walters Art
Museum; 19r Kingfisher Artbank; 20 iStock/Sami Suni; 21t Shutterstock/muratart;
21b Shutterstock/meunierd; 22 iStock/BrettCharlton; 23 iStock; 23t Walters Art Museum;
24 Alamy/Mr Steve Vidler; 25 Jastrow; 25b Alamy/Art Archive; 26–27 iStock/roc8jas; 26b Greg
Willis; 27 Shutterstock/S-F; 28–29 Alamy/APS(UK); 29 Kingfisher Artbank; 30–31 Shutterstock/
Mapics; 32 iStock/ArevHamb.
Cards: Front tl iStock/Gabriele Maltini; tr Shutterstock/Luciano Mortula; bl Shutterstock/Honzra
Hruby; br Shutterstock/WitR; Back tl iStock/allou; tr Shutterstock/Benedictus; bl iStock;
br Shutterstock/Reinhold Leitner.

You will find c. before some dates. This stands for *circa*, which means "about."

Front cover: The head of the goddess Sulis Minerva from the Temple Courtyard of
the Roman baths in Bath, UK.

CONTENTS

For your free audio download go to
www.panmacmillan.com/RemarkableRomans
or goo.gl/XnzDqC
Happy listening!

Who were the Romans?	4
Rome and its empire	6
Buying and selling	8
A mighty army	10
Gods and temples	12
At home	14
Food and feasts	16
Getting dressed	18
Thrills and spills	20
Going to the baths	22
Girls, boys, and toys	24
Pompeii	26
What happened to Rome?	28
Glossary	30
Index	32

Who were the Romans?

The Romans were the people who ruled a huge empire almost 2000 years ago. With the help of their armies, they spread their culture, language (Latin), building style, and systems of organization.

SPOTLIGHT: Roman Empire

Founded:	753 BCE
Ended:	476 CE
Language:	Latin
Location:	centered on modern-day Italy

The Romans built this aqueduct in southern France.

Today we can still find the remains of Roman walls and buildings—even public baths. We sometimes dig up old coins, pottery jars, or rings and brooches. These objects help us to understand how the Romans lived.

Elaborate jewelry, such as this pair of earrings, has been found at Roman sites.

Roman ruins near the town of Cordoba, in Spain.

Rome and its empire

More than 2700 years ago Rome was just a few villages. By 1 CE, Rome was the biggest city in the world. By 117 CE, Rome ruled an empire that covered Spain, France, Britain, parts of Germany, Romania, Greece, western Asia, and North Africa.

The Basilica Cistern in Constantinople (modern Istanbul) was built by the Roman Emperor Justinian.

Augustus changed the way Rome was ruled and became the first Roman emperor.

SPOTLIGHT: Emperor Augustus

Born:	63 BCE (as Gaius Octavius)
Died:	14 CE
Ruled:	27 BCE – 14 CE
Famous for:	first emperor of Rome

The Romans built straight roads across their empire.

FACT ...

Legend says that Rome was founded by Romulus who, with his twin brother Remus, had been brought up by a wolf.

Buying and selling

Every Roman city had a central place called the forum. People met here to do business and to visit the market and shops.

Romans used coins made of gold, silver, bronze, and copper.

the remains of the Forum in Rome

The Romans were great traders. At Roman ports, ships were loaded with pottery and cloth. Traders bought and sold sacks of grain, jars of wine, olive oil, and even people. These people were slaves who had no freedom and had to work hard for no money.

FACT ...

In 68 BCE pirates attacked the Roman port of Ostia. The Romans built 500 ships to fight them.

A mighty army

The Roman army was divided into groups called legions. Most soldiers fought on foot, but some fought on horseback. Roman soldiers wore tunics, sandals or boots, helmets, and body armor. Their weapons were short swords, daggers, and spears.

Soldiers in the Roman army fought battles in strict and highly organized formations.

a Roman general's helmet

One of the greatest Roman soldiers was the politician and general Julius Caesar. He became dictator of Rome before his enemies murdered him.

SPOTLIGHT: Julius Caesar

Born:	100 BCE
Died:	44 BCE (murdered)
Ruled:	45 – 44 BCE
Famous for:	first dictator of Rome

Julius Caesar marched into Rome and took over the government.

Gods and temples

The Romans believed in many different gods, including Jupiter (god of the sky), Juno (goddess of marriage), Diana (goddess of hunting), and Mars (god of war).

Jupiter   Neptune   Juno   Mars   Bacchus

Romans believed that the three-headed dog Cerberus guarded the door to the Underworld.

The Romans built temples and held festivals to honor their gods, and told myths about them. These stories also told of heroes and monsters.

The Pantheon Temple, Rome. Its domed ceiling (below) is nearly 2000 years old.

At home

The Romans built different kinds of houses. In the biggest cities, such as Rome or Ostia, people lived in multi-level apartment buildings, which often took up a whole city block. Many towns had family houses with a tiled roof, open courtyard, and pools of water.

Rich Romans lived in comfortable villas with spacious rooms and courtyard gardens.

The small windows had shutters.
In the country, rich people owned big
houses called villas. Some had fine
wall paintings, called frescoes, or floors
decorated with mosaics.

FACT ...

Romans believed that gods and spirits
protected their homes. People made
offerings to these gods every day.

Food and feasts

In the kitchens of the rich, slaves carried water and firewood. Pots and pans boiled on the brick stove. Cooks used olive oil, herbs, and spices. A main dish might be pork, fish, or chicken. Roman people ate onions, peas, and cabbages, as well as figs and grapes. They sweetened their food and drinks with honey.

Very rich people held banquets where everyone ate far too much food!

FACT...

Guests at a Roman banquet might eat mice cooked in honey, snails in wine, dumplings made with brains, or even boiled ostrich.

Wealthy Romans used silver tableware, while others used utensils made from bone or wood.

17

Getting dressed

A rich Roman woman would wear a
long tunic with a woolen dress called
a stola on top. She would use perfume
and jars of makeup, and curl her hair
and pile it up in the latest style. She
would check her appearance in a mirror
made of polished metal.

Rich women would have
bronze mirrors and
wooden combs.

Important men wore a heavy woolen robe called a toga. They wrapped it around themselves and then over one shoulder. Children, slaves, and working people all wore short tunics.

FACT ...

Wealthy Roman women covered their face with poisonous white lead to make themselves look pale.

Jewelry, such as this snake bracelet, was made from gold, pearls, and precious stones.

Thrills and spills

The Romans loved to watch violent and dangerous sports. At the Circus Maximus stadium in Rome, they could watch exciting chariot racing. At the Colosseum slaves and gladiators battled each other to the death. There were also wild animal fights and mock sea battles.

SPOTLIGHT: Colosseum, Rome

Built:	72–80 CE
Height:	165 ft. (50m)
Capacity:	50,000 people
Famous for:	the arena had 36 trap doors

Romans who wanted less bloodthirsty entertainment could enjoy funny plays (comedies) or sad ones (tragedies) at the theater.

Every city had an open-air theater called an amphitheater.

The most successful Roman charioteers became celebrities.

Going to the baths

Every Roman town had public baths for men and women. Romans went there every day to meet their friends and relax. They often started with some exercises or games. Then they would visit the pools, the hot tubs, the cold tubs, and steam rooms. Afterward, they might have a massage.

The remains of Roman heated flooring at Housesteads Roman fort, Northumberland, UK.

FACT...

At the baths, the Romans rubbed their body with oil and then scraped it clean with a tool called a strigil (right).

The Roman baths in Bath, UK were built over a natural hot spring.

Girls, boys, and toys

Roman babies played with clay rattles in the shape of animals. Toddlers played with marbles and dolls. At about seven years old, some boys and girls learned reading, writing, and arithmetic. They used a sharp point to scrape the letters on boards covered in wax. If they made a mistake, they smoothed over the wax and started again.

Romans played different games with counters on a square board.

Some boys from rich families learned about history, poetry, and making speeches. Some girls learned how to run a home, sew, and play a musical instrument.

a toy buffalo from Ancient Rome

FACT ...

At birth, Roman children were given a charm called a bulla. They wore it until they were 16 years old (boys) or married (girls).

Pompeii

In 79 CE, a volcano called Mount Vesuvius erupted with huge force. A cloud of superheated ash and rock poured from the volcano and buried the nearby town of Pompeii.

FACT...

The entrance of one house in Pompeii had a picture of a fierce dog with a notice saying "Beware of the dog."

SPOTLIGHT: Pompeii

Buried:	79 CE
Rediscovered:	1748 by Spaniard, Alcubierre
Population at time:	11,000 people
Importance:	preserved Roman town

Hundreds of years later, the rock was cleared away and workers found the buried Roman streets, houses, shops, markets, and theaters. They even found leftover food in pots and pans.

Many villas in Pompeii had colorful paintings on their walls.

What happened to Rome?

The Romans fought their enemies for hundreds of years. The Roman Empire became huge, but it was difficult to rule. Warriors attacked the forts along its borders, and some even attacked the city of Rome. The city became less powerful and was finally taken over by armies from the north of Europe.

An aerial view of Housesteads Fort on Hadrian's Wall, the northernmost border of the Roman Empire.

Important Dates in Ancient Rome

753 BCE   Rome begins

250 BCE   The Romans rule most of Italy

58–50 BCE Julius Caesar conquers Gaul (including
modern-day France)

27 BCE   Augustus becomes first Roman Emperor

43 CE   The Romans start to conquer Britain

79 CE   The volcano Vesuvius erupts in Italy

117 CE   The Roman Empire is at its largest

330 CE   Constantinople becomes capital of the
Roman Empire in the East

410 CE   Goths attack and capture Rome

476 CE   The Roman Empire in the West comes
to an end

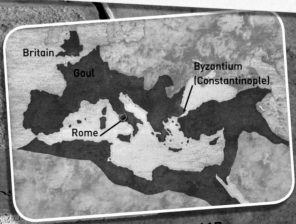

the Roman Empire in 117 CE

GLOSSARY

aqueduct A bridge that carries water.

BCE Short for "Before the Common Era" (any date before 1 CE). It is also sometimes known as BC (before Christ).

chariot A light, fast-moving carriage pulled by horses.

conquer To beat an enemy.

culture The ways of living of a particular group of people.

empire A group of countries ruled by one emperor.

erupt To explode violently.

forum The business center and meeting place in an Ancient Roman town.

legion A large battle unit in the Roman army.

massage Rubbing muscles to help relax the body.

mosaic A picture made up of small pieces of colored pottery, stone, or glass.

myth An old story about gods, goddesses, heroes, or monsters.

offering Something given to honor or please a god.

slave Someone who is not free and is forced to work for no money.

spirit A magical being who brings good or bad luck.

stola A long, pleated dress worn over a tunic.

toga A woolen robe worn by important men in Ancient Rome.

trader Someone who buys and sells goods to make money.

tunic A plain knee-length, sleeveless dress often worn by soldiers.

villa A large Roman house, usually in the countryside.

INDEX

aqueducts 4
armies 4, 10–11, 28
Augustus, Emperor 7, 29

Bath (England) 23
baths 5, 22–23
Britain 23, 28, 29

Caesar, Julius 11, 29
chariot racing 20–21
children 24–25
clothes 18–19
Colosseum, the 20
Constantinople 6, 29

education 25

food 16–17
forts 22, 28

gladiators 20
gods 12–13, 15

houses 14–15, 27

jewelry 5, 19

money 8, 9

Pantheon, the 13
pirates 9
Pompeii 26–27

roads 7
Roman Empire, the 4, 6, 28, 29
Rome 4, 6, 7, 8, 11, 14
ruins 2, 5, 8, 26–27, 28–29

slaves 9, 16, 19, 20
soldiers 10–11

temples 13
theaters 21, 27
toys 24, 25
trade 8–9

villas 14–15

REMARKABLE ROMANS

Collector Card

REMARKABLE ROMANS

Collector Card

REMARKABLE ROMANS

Collector Card

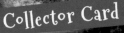

REMARKABLE ROMANS

Collector Card

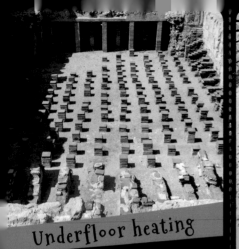

Underfloor heating

Luxury heated flooring blasted hot air to heat villas and public baths.

SCORE

IN USE TODAY: no, but ruins remain	4
IMPORTANCE: luxury	2
WORLD FIRST: possibly	8
ROMAN FIRST: 15 BCE	1

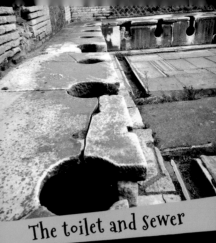

The toilet and sewer

Public toilets were built over running water and joined a network of sewers.

SCORE

IN USE TODAY: Cloaca Maxima sewer	3
IMPORTANCE: desirable	8
WORLD FIRST: no, but used extensively	3
ROMAN FIRST: 500 BCE	9

Public baths

All Romans could wash, swim, meet friends, or relax at luxury public baths.

SCORE

IN USE TODAY: modern spas; ruins	2
IMPORTANCE: good for public health	5
WORLD FIRST: as baths for all	7
ROMAN FIRST: 20 BCE	2

The newspaper

The world's first daily newspaper was probably Rome's *Acta Diurna*.

SCORE

IN USE TODAY: newspapers in general	6
IMPORTANCE: useful communication	3
WORLD FIRST: first daily news	9
ROMAN FIRST: 130 BCE	4